Living the Story

What it was like to be there

Dramas

that bring

the Bible

alive

J U D I T H   R O S S A L L

kevin mayhew

First published in 2003 by
KEVIN MAYHEW LTD
Buxhall, Stowmarket, Suffolk, 1P14 3BW
E-mail: info@kevinmayhewltd.com

KINGSGATE PUBLISHING INC
1000 Pannell Street, Suite G, Columbia, MO 65201
E-mail: sales@kingsgatepublishing.com

9 8 7 6 5 4 3 2 1 0

ISBN 1 84417 101 9
Catalogue Number 1500602

Cover design by Jonathan Stroulger
Typesetting by Louise Selfe
Printed in Great Britain

Contents

Introduction

In 1984 I heard a series of sermons which changed my view of Scripture and the way in which I read it from that point on. The subject was almost always a Gospel story and the preacher concentrated not simply on telling us what the passage meant but on inviting us to live the story alongside the disciples. It was so brilliantly done that in my mind the disciples became real people with real hopes and fears, problems and joys, and there was tremendous encouragement in the realisation that they had struggled as I do. I began to recognise that in the Scriptures we have a large number of stories in which people grapple with the ups and downs of life and faith, but that much of the preaching that I had heard to that point concentrated on presenting propositions. Ever since then I have tried to make a regular habit of reading Scripture while imagining what it was like to be one of the people who is a part of the story. And I have tried to reflect that sense of the power of the story in my preaching and leading of worship.

This is, of course, hardly original, and there are many books around which urge us to do just that. But I mention it because that experience and that way of reading Scripture has shaped this book and its contents. In one way or another, every piece offered here started with the question, 'What was it like to be there?' Sometimes, I moved a long way from that question by the time I reached the finished meditation or drama, but not, I hope, so far that the original intent is totally lost.

The majority of pieces offered are drama scripts; they have nearly all been used in services that I have led at Guildford Methodist Church or around our Circuit. (The exception to this occurred when I finally came up with an idea for how the Easter story could be told in drama, on Easter Monday this year!) On the whole, the scripts were written with the intention of introducing or beginning to open up a particular passage. Just occasionally, allowing one character to tell their story proved to be so powerful that I let the drama stand on its own without a sermon. Normally, however, the drama was intended to do no more than introduce the theme of the service and I have in each case indicated what that original theme was.

The meditations were also used in services and almost always they replaced the sermon. The services in which they were used usually involved a fair amount of silence and some meditative music. We normally distributed orders of service, which made it clear that the same event would be described through the eyes of different people who were present. I have found that presenting several different perspectives has helped the story to come to life. The very fact that the different speakers see things slightly differently invites people to ask themselves what they would have seen and understood had they been there. I have tried to ensure that each of the different speakers helps to build a complete picture; for that reason I would urge that the meditations be used as written with all three versions of the story being read at the same service or other event.

Naturally, my imagining of a story will differ from other people's and it may well seem to some that I have missed the real meaning. But even if that is the case, I still hope that the work presented here can provoke people to visualise for themselves the events described in Scripture and can help them to their own sense of being part of the great story of faith.

Judith Rossall

Now you're sixty-four

Theme
Sarah has to be persuaded that a baby is a good idea at her age.

Introduction
Abraham, like Jesus, saw himself as called to serve. He may have got the child he always wanted, but he did not get an easy life! This drama explores the challenges he faced. What matters is that people get the idea that years passed between the promise of the baby and Isaac's arrival. To achieve this you can simply have Abram and Sarai walk across the stage carrying various posters.

Scripture reference
Genesis 12:1-20 (and most of the following chapters!)

The Lord had said to Abram, 'Leave your country, your people and your father's household and go to the land I will show you.' (Genesis 12:1)

Characters
Narrator
Abram
Sarai

Now you're sixty-four

Narrator   Ladies and gentlemen, we proudly present for your delectation and delight a story which will enthral and thrill you. An epic story of love, faith and hope such as you have never heard before. I present our hero, Abram.

Enter Abram.

Narrator   Naturally our hero fulfils all the requirements of an epic story. He is handsome and strong. *(Abram preens)* He is wise and knowledgeable. *(Abram produces a Bible and studies it)* He is young and adventurous. *(Abram walks over to Narrator and whispers in his ear)* How old?

Abram   Seventy-five.

Narrator   Are you sure?

Abram   Well I don't actually have a birth certificate you understand, since they haven't been invented yet. But I do know how old I am!

Narrator   Oh, OK. Well, we'd better carry on. Go back to your place and try to look adventurous.

Abram returns to his place and strikes a classic strongman pose, i.e. both arms outstretched and bent at the elbow.

Narrator   I said adventurous.

Abram shrugs.

Narrator   And, ladies and gentlemen, I present our heroine. *(enter Sarai who stands a few paces to Abram's left)* A fit companion for our hero in every way. She is beautiful and strong *(Sarai preens)*, wise and knowledgeable *(Sarai walks over to Abram and they study the Bible together)* and young *(Narrator breaks off and looks at Abram. Abram shakes his head)* . . . at heart. *(Sarai puts hands on hips and glares at Abram, she walks back to her original place)* She is adventurous? *(looks* *over to Abram who shakes his head again)* Oh well, on with the story. One day our hero had a vision.

Abram   Sarai, I've had a vision.

Sarai   That's nice, dear.

Abram   God is going to make me a great nation and bless the entire world through me!

Sarai   That's nice, dear.

Abram   So we have to go to a new land.

Sarai   That's nice, dear. Hang on a minute. We have to go to a new land?

Abram   Well, yes. You have to come with me.

Sarai   And how far away is this new land exactly?

Abram   I don't know.

Sarai   *(produces large book labelled The Known World from Ur to Canaan)* Let's look it up. What did you say it is called?

Abram   I don't know.

Sarai   Well, where is it?

Abram   I don't know that either.

Sarai   What do you know about it?

Abram   Not a lot really.

Sarai   *(in a reasonable voice)* Then how are we going to know when we get there?

Abram   God will tell me, I suppose.

Sarai   Abram, do you even know how long it is likely to be before we come back home again?

Abram   Yes, I do, but you aren't going to like it.

Narrator So, filled with a spirit of adventure, our hero and heroine eagerly set out upon their quest. *(Abram marches off to his right, leaving Sarai with her arms folded and tapping her foot; Narrator pointedly repeats)* Our hero and heroine set out on their quest. *(Abram comes back and beckons; Sarai shakes her head; Narrator walks over to Sarai)* Sarai, you have to go with him.

Sarai   Do I? Why?

Narrator Because in your day women were submissive and they did what their husbands told them to.

Sarai   Even when he wanted to set off on some great journey, not knowing where he's going or even how he will know when he's arrived?

Narrator Even then, yes.

Sarai   Even when the only reason he's doing this is because he thinks he had a vision from God?

Narrator Even then, yes.

Sarai   It was pretty tough being a woman in my day, wasn't it?

Narrator All right, you have to go because Abram needs you. In order to become a great nation he needs to have a son. He's going to find that pretty difficult without you.

Sarai   He's going to find it pretty difficult with me. Do you know how old he is?

Narrator He did mention it, yes.

Sarai   I'm only ten years younger you know. At our age we should be retiring, putting our feet up, enjoying the grandchildren. Not setting out on a Divine Mystery Tour. In fact, it's time I got a pension.

Narrator   Well, unfortunately, Haran, in 4000 BC, was a little lacking in State Benefits. You don't have any choice. You have to go with Abram.

Sarai   Oh all right then. *(she moves very reluctantly towards Abram. The Narrator returns to his place)*

Narrator   Where was I? Oh, yes. So, filled with a spirit of adventure, our hero and heroine eagerly set out upon their quest. *(Abram marches from right to left looking enthusiastic, followed several paces later by Sarai, wandering along with her hands in her pockets muttering things like, 'typical man, doesn't even know where he's going'; eventually they return to their original positions)* One day our hero had a vision.

Abram   Sarai, I've had a vision.

Sarai   That's nice, dear.

Abram   God spoke to me.

Sarai   That's nice, dear. I don't suppose he mentioned a pension, did he?

Abram   He's going to give us this land.

Sarai   That's nice, dear. Hang on a minute. He's going to give us this land, as in Canaan?

Abram   That's right, Canaan. Or as I like to call it, 'the Promised Land'.

Sarai   Abram, it may have escaped your notice, but the Canaanites are already in Canaan. If we try and take it, I think they might object.

Abram   God is going to give it to our descendants, my dear.

Sarai   Oh, that's all right then.

Abram   *(surprised at her acceptance)* It is?

Sarai	Well, of course it is. We don't actually have any descendants, and we aren't likely to get any at our age. Even the Canaanites can't start an argument with someone who doesn't actually exist.
Abram	Sarai, I don't think that's quite what God meant.
Narrator	So Abram and Sarai travelled on. *(Sarai and Abram start to walk as before; they follow exactly the same route but this time when they return to their original positions, Sarai holds up a sign saying 'Twenty-five years later')*
Sarai	That was a long journey. Where are we now?
Abram	In Hebron dear.
Sarai	Hebron? Isn't that in Canaan?
Abram	*(reluctantly)* It might be.
Sarai	You mean we've travelled all this way and ended up back in Canaan?
Narrator	*(hastily)* One day our hero had a vision.
Abram	Sarai, I've had a vision.
Sarai	That's nice, dear. Or is it?
Abram	We're going to have a son!
	Silence
Abram	Isn't that wonderful news, dear?
Sarai	Abram, you were 100 last birthday. And I was 90. Don't you think we're getting a little old to have children?
Abram	It's going to be a miracle child.
Sarai	And who exactly is going to feed this miracle child? And change its nappy? And get up with it in the middle of the night?

Abram   We'll be so pleased to be parents, I'm sure we won't mind at all.

Sarai   That will be a miracle! Abram, since God is going to work a miracle for us, could you ask him if we could skip straight to the grandchildren; I hear they're much more fun. In fact, really, we're about the right age for great-grandchildren if you think about it.

Abram   But we are going to have a child. And we will always know that this child was a gift of God. Of course we are far too old to be parents – that's the point. This child will be born only by the power of God, because God is starting something new with us. A new people who will know that they owe their very existence to God. A new nation who will know that they have their land only because God gave it to them. And I don't know how, but somehow from what God is doing today, through us, will come something or someone that will be a blessing for the whole world.

Sarai   *(doubtfully)* Well, if you put it like that.

Abram   Sarai, we are going to be just one small part of God's plan. We can't turn away from this chance. Look at it this way – with a bit of luck he'll be off our hands before your 110th birthday.

Redus bushicus

Theme
Moses pops into his local garden centre in search of another talking bush.

Introduction
This drama highlights how difficult it was for Moses to listen to what God was saying. It can also be used as a general introduction to his story.

Scripture reference
Exodus 3:1-15

But Moses said to God, 'Who am I, that I should go to Pharaoh and bring the Israelites out of Egypt?' (Exodus 3:11)

Characters
Moses, a shepherd and reluctant prophet
Sarah, a gardener

Redus bushicus

Sarah is tending a red plant. There is a sign saying 'Rachael and daughter: Gardeners to Pharaoh'.

Enter Moses.

Sarah   Evening, can I help you?

Moses   Good evening. Um, I was hoping to talk to someone who could advise me about plants.

Sarah   Then you've come to the right place. I'm Sarah and what I don't know about plants isn't worth knowing.

Moses   Oh, good. *(silence)* Moses looks at his shoes while Sarah looks at him expectantly.

Sarah   So what would you like to know?

Moses   Well . . . *(looks up and spots the plant)* Oh, what a lovely plant!

Sarah   Thank you, this is a redus bushicus. A particularly fine specimen, if I say so myself.

Moses   It's very red, isn't it?

Sarah   It's supposed to be red, sir.

Moses   Yes, but if a person were to, say, come across it in a desert, and if that person just happened to be very tired and not thinking straight, well, that person might just think it's on fire, mightn't they?

Sarah   *(looks at the bush and then says doubtfully)* I don't think so, sir, not really.

Moses   And then the strange thing would be, that it seemed to be on fire but not actually burning up. And it would be understandable if a person got confused, wouldn't it?

Sarah   It's just a red plant, sir. Someone would have to be very confused to think it was on fire. Not to mention a bit thick!

Moses   Drat!

Sarah   Was there anything else, sir?

Moses   Do you, er, do you ever talk to your plants?

Sarah   Oh yes, all the time. It encourages them to grow, you know!

Moses   I don't suppose any of them ever answered you back, did they?

Sarah   *(firmly)* No!

Moses   Drat!

Sarah   You don't know a lot about plants, do you, sir?

Moses   Not really, I'm a shepherd, not a gardener.

Sarah   I can assure you that every plant I've ever come across has been distinctly on the silent side. A little rustling in the breeze – that might happen. But if you want conversation over the dinner table, you're better off looking elsewhere. One of your sheep might be more useful.

Moses   And you've never had one spontaneously combust?

Sarah   No sir.

Moses   Or order you to remove your shoes?

Sarah   Definitely not!

Moses   Drat!

Sarah   Do I take it you have, sir? Had a plant spontaneously combust and order you to remove your shoes, I mean.

Moses   Well, I think so. You see, I was in the desert and there was this bush . . .

Sarah   It spoke to you, I take it?

Moses   Afraid so.

Sarah   And what did it say? Other than 'Oi you, take your shoes off.'

Moses   It said, 'I am the God of your Father, the God of Abraham, the God of Isaac and the God of Jacob.'

Sarah   I see. It was suffering from a slight delusion of grandeur really, wasn't it, this bush? Being able to talk has obviously given it ideas.

Moses   Either that, or it really was God.

Sarah   That would be the other option, yes.

Moses   But it's much more likely that it was just an ordinary bush.

Sarah   *(sarcastically)* Just an ordinary talking bush. Absolutely, sir. Happens all the time! Did it say anything else?

Moses   It wants me to go to Pharaoh and tell him to set the Israelites free.

Sarah   Oh, so this conversing shrubbery doesn't just have delusions of grandeur, it's also suicidal! How nice. Did it offer to go with you?

Moses   Sort of. It said that it would bring us to the Promised Land.

Sarah   Which is no doubt populated by lots of other bits of chattering greenery!

Moses   No, just flowing with milk and honey.

Sarah   Delightful, I'm sure. I'm still not sure how I can be of help.

Moses   Well, I was hoping that you might be able to tell me about a talking plant really – but obviously not.

Sarah   *(firmly)* No, sir. Now is there anything else?

Moses	Do you have a walking stick?
Sarah	*(suspiciously)* Yes.
Moses	I don't suppose you've ever dropped it and had it suddenly turn into a snake, have you?
Sarah	No, sir.
Moses	Or developed an instant case of leprosy?
Sarah	No, Sir.
Moses	Drat!
Sarah	I think you might need to face facts, sir. Brilliant as my plants are, none of them can burn without being consumed, talk, or turn walking sticks into snakes. It looks as though this may well have been God.
Moses	Yes, but if it was God, I'm going to have do what he said, aren't I? It must have been the bush. Are you sure you know all the bushes in the world.
Sarah	Not all of them, no, sir.
Moses	Well, then. It was probably just a new variety of bush that you've never heard of!
Sarah	Oh, I think I would have heard about this one, sir. We gardeners like to keep each other informed and if someone had managed to grow a talking bush, news would have spread.
Moses	Drat!
Sarah	So are you going to do it then? Go and see Pharaoh, I mean.
Moses	*(sounding miserable)* I'm going to have to, aren't I?
Sarah	Well, the way I see it, if God wants you to do something, he'll help you out, won't he? I mean, there's not a lot of point sending you in if you're just going to get killed, is there?

Moses   *(still miserable)* I guess not.

Sarah   You're going to have trust God on this one.

Moses   Goodbye then.

Sarah   Goodbye and good luck.

Exit Moses.

Sarah   *(tending to the plant and talks to it)* Honestly! The things God has to do to get people's attention! A talking bush – whatever next? Food dropping out of the sky, do you think? It would be so much easier if people would just listen! *(leans closer)* I'm sorry, what was that you said?

To be sure

Theme
Gideon has to be persuaded that fighting the Midianites is a good idea.

Introduction
This drama explores the theme of knowing what God wants us to do. In particular it highlights, from Gideon's story, the idea that sometimes our difficulty is that God's will is clear, but we are unwilling to obey.

Scripture reference
Judges 6:11-40

Gideon said to God, 'If you will save Israel by my hand as you have promised – look, I will place a wool fleece on the threshing floor. If there is dew only on the fleece and all the ground is dry, then I will know that you will save Israel by my hand, as you said.' And that is what happened. Gideon rose early the next day; he squeezed the fleece and wrung out the dew – a bowlful of water. (Judges 6:36)

Characters
Narrator
Gabriel *(wearing a halo and either robes or a big sign saying 'The Archangel Gabriel' and a badge saying 3,123,201 TODAY!)*
Gideon *(wearing a jacket – sheepskin if possible)*

To be sure

Hide a large water gun near where Gabriel will stand and a hairdryer for the Narrator and a sword for Gideon.

Narrator   From the beginning of time people have wondered, 'Is God speaking to me? How do I know if he is? What is the will of God for my life? Will England win the next World Cup?'

Gideon   *(from off stage)* Get on with it, will you?

Narrator   Sorry! And so we present to you the story of one man who wanted to find out the will of God. Many years ago Israel was being oppressed by the Midianites. If the Israelites planted some crops, the Midianites would invade and ruin them. The Israelites were so afraid that they hid in mountains and caves and they prayed to God to free them from their oppressors. And God chose one man, Gideon, to free the Israelites.

Enter Gideon, walking tall and looking pleased with himself.

Narrator   Gideon was a mighty warrior. *(Gideon nods and takes up a classic strong-man pose)* Strong and fearless, he would die for his country. *(Gideon looks over to the Narrator, now less sure)* If the enemy tortured him, plucked out his eyes, cut out his tongue what did it matter? *(Gideon now looking very nervous, walks over to Narrator)* As long as he could serve God. *(Gideon taps Narrator on shoulder)* Yes?

Gideon   You are exaggerating, aren't you? About the torture bit, I mean.

Narrator   What do you care, you're a strong and mighty warrior, aren't you?

Gideon   Yes, but I don't want to get hurt.

Narrator   Can we get on with this?

Gideon reluctantly returns to his place. Throughout the next conversation he stares at the floor and sulks.

Narrator   One day God sent Gideon a message.

Enter Gabriel to the sound of 'Happy Birthday to You.' He grins, obviously enjoying himself. He stands on the other side of the Narrator to Gideon.

Gabriel   Guess what?

Narrator   You'd like to get straight on with the story.

Gabriel   *(like a sulky 5-year-old)* No, go on, take a guess . . .

Narrator   I can't think.

Gabriel   *(like an enthusiastic 5-year-old)* It's my birthday!

Narrator   *(sarcastically)* I'd never have known. *(to the audience)* One day God sent Gideon a message.

Gabriel   *(ignoring this)* I got some excellent presents.

Narrator   *(diverted)* Presents? What presents do you give an angel? New halo is it?

Gabriel   This old thing! I've had this for years.

Narrator   A new cloud to sit on?

Gabriel   I'm quite happy with my Nebulous 2000, thank you. No, I got this. *(produces large water gun and sprays the audience)* Good, isn't it?

Narrator   *(looks at gun and sighs)* Can we get on with the story now? *(to the audience)* One day God sent Gideon a message. He told him to go and fight the Midianites.

Gabriel   *(leans past the Narrator to address Gideon and says very casually)* Gideon, go and fight the Midianites. *(he squirts the congregation again, and grins, clearly more interested in his new toy than anything else; Narrator glares at him, he hangs his head)*

Gideon   *(to Narrator and sounding very worried)* You are sure I'm not going to get hurt, aren't you?

Narrator   Will you get on with it?

Gideon   *(suddenly thinks)* But how do I know this is a message from God? *(looks over at Gabriel)* You could be anybody. I need to be sure.

Narrator   *(who is not expecting this)* How many angels carrying a supersoaker have you met?

Gideon   I'm not doing anything until I'm sure that this message is from God. *(kneels down and prays)* Oh Lord, so that I may know that it is you speaking, please send a miracle. I will lay my fleece on the floor tonight. If in the morning I find that the fleece is wet but the ground is dry, then I will know that you want me to fight the Midianites. *(takes off jacket and lays it on the floor, then lies down and goes to sleep)*

Narrator and Gabriel look at each other in disgust.

Narrator   Now what do we do?

Gabriel   I don't know.

They stand for a moment and then both look at the water gun at the same time. They look at each other and grin.

Narrator   Of course!

Gabriel wanders up to the jacket whistling and trying to look innocent. Sprays the jacket with the water pistol then wanders back to his place. Hides the pistol behind his back.

Narrator   And in the morning . . .

Gideon wakes up and checks the jacket and floor.

Gideon   The fleece is wet and the floor is dry!

Narrator and Gabriel   It's a miracle!

Gideon   Drat! *(thinks for a moment, then says hopefully)* But it could be a coincidence!

Narrator   You're kidding! *(throughout next speech stands with hands on hips looking annoyed)*

Gideon   *(praying)* O Lord, so that I may be truly sure of your will, please send another miracle. I will lay my fleece on the floor again and if in the morning I find that the fleece is dry and the floor is wet, then I will fight the Midianites. *(goes back to sleep)*

Narrator   *(to Gabriel, sounding annoyed)* Come on then.

Narrator produces hairdryer and they dry the jacket. Gabriel carefully squirts around the edge of the jacket and finally squirts Gideon who wakes up.

Narrator   And in the morning . . .

Gideon   The ground is wet and the fleece is dry.

Narrator and Gabriel   It's a miracle!

Gideon   I'm going to get hurt, aren't I?

Narrator   So Gideon fought the Midianites. *(Gideon picks up sword and wanders off looking very reluctant)*

Gabriel   And it was a mighty victory.

Gideon   *(from off stage still sounding reluctant)* Hurray.

Narrator and Gabriel   The End.

Narrator leaves. Gabriel stays to squirt a few more members of the congregation. Narrator reappears and drags him off.

Facing the enemy

Theme

Saul, Eliab and David describe their feelings on facing Goliath.

Introduction

In September 2001 our church was part-way through a series of sermons on the story of David. The Sunday after 11 September we were due to look at the story of David and Goliath. After some considerable thought and prayer, I decided to stay with the theme and to use the story to allow some of the characters involved to express their doubts and faith, in the belief that people in the congregation would share many of the same feelings. The result was the meditations given below.

Scripture reference

1 Samuel 17:1-50

Early in the morning David left the flock with a shepherd, loaded up and set out, as Jesse had directed. He reached the camp as the army was going out to its battle positions, shouting the war cry. Israel and the Philistines were drawing up their lines facing each other. David left his things with the keeper of supplies, ran to the battle lines and greeted his brothers. As he was talking with them, Goliath, the Philistine champion from Gath, stepped out from his lines and shouted his usual defiance, and David heard it. When the Israelites saw the man, they all ran from him in great fear. (1 Samuel 17:20-24)

Characters

Saul (King of Israel)
Eliab (David's brother)
David

Facing the enemy

Saul How can life suddenly have come to this?

I thought I was the Lord's anointed, I thought that would make me invulnerable. Others looked at me and rejoiced. 'There is no one else like him among all the people,' they cried. I was their saviour and their hero. It seemed I could do no wrong.

I now feel only shock and terror. The mighty Saul is faced with an enemy I do not know how to handle. The others are no longer saying, 'There is no one else like him,' instead they whisper behind my back that I have lost my way and no longer know how to lead. My position and my leadership are threatened and, worse than that, I am no longer sure that I can protect the innocent who rely on me.

And I wonder if God has deserted me. Prophets have warned before that in my power and self-satisfaction I was no longer listening to God as I should. Samuel confronted me when I chose to keep the spoils of war rather than obey the commands of God. But is my sin so great that it deserves this? Is my failure so awful that others should die and be enslaved for it? Where is the God who promised to be with us, and why is he letting this happen?

And so in my confusion I hide in my tent. My advisors come and we hold meeting after meeting, knowing that others await our decisions. Knowing that we must confront our enemy, but not knowing how. And all the time wondering.

I never realised that life can change like this.

Eliab I am so afraid and so angry and I do not know what to do.

I used to look to Saul and be so sure that he would lead us. He's beaten the Philistines before; he has rescued cities and routed armies. So why now does he shake with fear before one single giant?

Everyone can see his fear and his shame. 'The king is pale and shaking' they say. 'He does not know how to respond. Where once he came out to lead us and prepare us for battle, now he keeps to his tent and all Israel knows that he is allowing the Philistines to mock us.'

The child in me just wants life to go back to what it was before. When I had a hero to look up to and certainties I could rely on. When we were the Lord's people and were sure that he would always rescue us.

And my fear makes me angry. I have to do something, hit out at someone. David was just in the way. Someone smaller and weaker than me on whom I could take it out. 'Who is this uncircumcised Philistine to defy the armies of the living God?' he demanded. A naive young idiot with no concept of what we were facing, daring to imply a criticism of us, the seasoned soldiers who have fought in battles while he was looking after sheep. Calling us cowards for not taking up the challenge. Implying that there was a simple solution to our dilemma. What does he want? That one of us accepts certain death and the rest of us become slaves? Of course I shouted, any human being would. Of course I got angry, how else am I to cope with my fear. Life will never be the same again and I do not know how to cope.

And so I sit and watch the giant mock us and I wonder what to do.

I am so afraid, I am so angry and I am so lost.

David I do not understand how we have come to this. I entered the camp to find the enemy mocking us and the army that defends my people in disarray. The Philistine is confident, laughing, sneering at our fear. The Lord's people tremble and no one will step forward to defend the honour of the living God.

I am angry and afraid and I want to hit out. I'm angry at those who are supposed to be defending us, who are doing nothing. And I'm angry at the enemy who mocks everything I believe in.

And if no one else will act then I will. If no one else will stand for our faith and our nation and our trust in God, then I will.

I am a boy, I am young and inexperienced and vulnerable. He is an adult, full grown. He is a soldier and he seems indestructible. This is not what I wanted, this is not a battle I would have chosen, but if this is what life forces on me, this is what I will do. I will call on what experience I do have, I will trust my God and I will do what I have to do.

So I will take my pitiful weapons and look to my powerful God. I do not know how we came to this, I only know this: I serve the God of love who walks with me even through the valley of death. I fear no evil when he is with me, when his rod and his staff comfort me. His goodness and his love follow me and I will dwell in his house for ever.

No harm done?

or, Why 'prophetting' is a dangerous business

Theme
Nathan's wife tries to persuade him not to confront King David.

Introduction
By looking at the confrontation between David and Nathan, following David's adultery with Bathsheba, this drama explores the need for everyone, no matter how powerful, to submit to God.

Scripture reference
2 Samuel 12:1-15

The Lord sent Nathan to David. When he came to him, he said, 'There were two men in a certain town, one rich and the other poor. The rich man had a very large number of sheep and cattle, but the poor man had nothing except one little ewe lamb he had bought. He raised it, and it grew up with him and his children. It shared his food, drank from his cup and even slept in his arms. It was like a daughter to him. Now a traveller came to the rich man, but the rich man refrained from taking one of his own sheep or cattle to prepare a meal for the traveller who had come to him. Instead, he took the ewe lamb that belonged to the poor man and prepared it for the one who had come to him.'

David burned with anger against the man and said to Nathan, 'As surely as the Lord lives, the man who did this deserves to die! He must pay for that lamb four times over, because he did such a thing and had no pity.'

Then Nathan said to David, 'You are the man!' (2 Samuel 12:1-7)

Characters
Nathan, a prophet
Abigail, his previously totally unheard-of wife

No harm done?

Nathan sits at a table, writing, while Abigail dusts around him (she could dust him and his book at some point). She pays Nathan little real attention at first.

Abigail   *(hums)*

Nathan   Excuse me.

Abigail   *(continues to hum)*

Nathan   *(louder)* Excuse me Abigail dear, could you hum a little quieter? I'm trying to work here.

Abigail   Oh, I'm sorry dear, I didn't realise you were prophetting!

Nathan   Prophetting?

Abigail   Yes, you know, you're a prophet, so what else does a prophet do but a little prophetting?

Nathan   *(sighs)* That's prophesying dear, a prophet prophesies!

Abigail   Yes, whatever. *(she carries on dusting without humming, then asks without much interest)* Are you prophesying anything interesting, dear?

Nathan   I've got a message for David.

Abigail   My brother David?

Nathan   No, not that David.

Abigail   Ah well, very common name David. Got even commoner now the King's called David. Why, I must have been to three circumcisions for little Davids in the last six months.

Nathan   Yes, well . . .

Abigail   So are you going to tell him anything interesting, this David?

Nathan   Well, it's about this woman he's met . . .

Abigail   *(instantly loses all interest in the housework, grabs a chair, sits down next to Nathan and asks with full attention)* Yes?

Nathan   *(a little disconcerted by her sudden interest)* Are you sure you want to hear this?

Abigail   Oh yes, how did he meet her?

Nathan   Well David is . . . *(he glances anxiously at Abigail, who is now watching him keenly)* . . . the, um, a soldier.

Abigail   Oh, I love a man in uniform.

Nathan   He wasn't in uniform when he met her.

Abigail   *(now very interested in the gossip)* Really! Do tell me more.

Nathan   I mean he wasn't on the front line. He was having a holiday, left everyone else to it and came home.

Abigail   *(a little disappointed)* Oh! Well, no harm done. I mean war must get boring, all that raping and pillaging. I've never seen the attraction myself! Now, how did he meet the woman?

Nathan   He saw her while she was taking a bath.

Abigail   Really! And how did he manage that? Forget to lock the bathroom door, did she?

Nathan   Not quite, he was on his roof and she was on hers, apparently.

Abigail   I see, quite the little exhibitionist then, isn't she. Still, so he had a little peek, no harm done there then.

Nathan   He did a bit more than peek . . .

Abigail   No, no, don't tell me, he coveted her, didn't he? I don't know, you prophetting types. I've always thought that commandment about 'Thou shalt not covet' was a bit excessive myself. So he coveted her – no harm done, really, is there?

Nathan   Abigail, he slept with her!

Abigail   Really! Still, boys will be boys, it's not too bad a sin is it? A little bit of repentance and everything will be all right – no harm done really.

Nathan   She was married.

Abigail   Really? Was the husband very upset?

Nathan   The husband is dead!

Abigail   Oh honestly, Nat, you didn't mention she was a widow! No harm done there then!

Nathan   She wasn't a widow when she met David.

Abigail   *(nods happily and then realises what he means)* Really! You mean he *(she makes a slitting gesture across her own throat)* . . .

Nathan   Well, let's just say he made the arrangements, shall we? And he married her pretty quickly afterwards.

Abigail   Ohh! *(thinks for a minute; while she is quiet, Nathan goes back to writing)* So, Nathan?

Nathan   *(without looking up)* Yes?

Abigail   This prophetting that you're doing.

Nathan   *(glances up)* It's not called . . . oh, never mind. *(goes back to his writing)*

Abigail   Nathan, you are going to be tactful, aren't you?

Nathan   *(looks up again)* Excuse me?

Abigail   When you do your prophetting bit. You are going to be tactful about it. After all, from what you say the last man to get in his way *(she makes the slitting gesture again)* . . .

Nathan   Abigail, how would you like me to be tactful about calling him an adulterous murderer?

Abigail *(thinks)* I know, why don't you sympathise with him about the little accident that happened to his wife's first husband and suggest that it might be an idea if it didn't happen again?

Nathan No!

Abigail Then why don't you tell him that he's a very good soldier, congratulate him on his success with the ladies and suggest he might like to stick to killing the enemy in future?

Nathan No!

Abigail Or why don't you . . .

Nathan *(interrupting her)* Abigail, I'm a prophet; I'm not paid to wrap things up nicely.

Abigail You're not paid at all, remember?

Nathan Ah yes, well. But the point is, Abigail, I have to be blunt, or he might not get the point.

Abigail *(sounding worried)* If you're too blunt he might show you the point . . . of his sword.

Nathan Abigail, don't worry, I'm going to be subtle about it. I'm going to gently ease into the subject.

Abigail *(starts calmly and becomes more annoyed as the sentence goes on)* And I'm sure he'll be very subtle in return as he gently eases his axe into your neck.

Nathan *(ignoring her)* I'm going to start with a story about some men who owned some sheep. He'll like that, he used to be a shepherd.

Abigail Oh, that's all right then . . . a shepherd turned soldier who . . . Hang on a minute.

Nathan *(realises that she has guessed)* Anyway, I must be going.

He jumps up, grabs his book and makes for the door; Abigail moves to block his exit and throughout the following he keeps trying unsuccessfully to get past her

Abigail	Used to be a shepherd, did he?
Nathan	Yes, dear.
Abigail	But now he's a soldier.
Nathan	Yes, dear.
Abigail	Except he's recently had a holiday.
Nathan	Yes, dear.
Abigail	And got married.
Nathan	Yes, dear.
Abigail	And his wife was very recently widowed.
Nathan	Yes, dear.
Abigail	And now she's pregnant?
Nathan	Yes, dear.
Abigail	Very royal sounding name isn't it, David?
Nathan	If you say so, dear.
Abigail	He wouldn't be known for his dislike of tall Philistines, would he, this David?
Nathan	He might be . . .
Abigail	Nathan, I put up with a lot, you know. When you gave up your nice steady job working for Benjamin Josephson, did I say anything?
Nathan	No, dear.
Abigail	'I'm going to work for someone much greater than Mr Josephson,' you said, failing to mention that the someone was God, whose idea of payment for a hard day's prophetting is another vision. We can't live on visions, can we, Nathan?

Nathan   No, dear.

Abigail   So I have one simple request. I understand that you need to prophet, but if you have to denounce someone's sins, why pick on the King. What about somebody who's still a shepherd? Why, that Samuel Jacobson will do, everyone knows that he's been known to filch the odd lamb for himself – why not go and denounce him?

Nathan   But David's done something much worse than that.

Abigail   But Samuel Jacobson isn't likely to have you thrown into jail or have your head cut off, is he?

Nathan   But God's law applies to everyone, whoever they are. God doesn't play favourites, so neither should I.

Abigail   All right, all right, I'll visit you in jail. I'll try to make sure that I bury your head with the rest of you, if that's what you really want.

Nathan   *(winces at the above statement)* It won't be like that. His Majesty and I will have a calm and rational discussion about the problem.

Abigail   Oh yes, he's known for his calm rationality, is our King.

Nathan   Abigail, I have to do this. David is as much a servant of God as everyone else. And God has told me to remind everyone to follow his law, whether they are King or pauper. *(he exits)*

Abigail shakes her head and then picks up the book from the table, holding it so that the congregation can see that 'The Word of God' is printed on it. She exits in the opposite direction to Nathan.

What did he say?

Theme
Two Israelites listen in on Isaiah's latest prophecy.

Introduction
A drama for Advent, looking at the idea that the Messiah will be David's descendant.

Scripture reference
Isaiah 9-11

For to us a child is born,
to us a son is given,
and the government will be on his shoulders.
And he will be called
Wonderful Counsellor, Mighty God,
Everlasting Father, Prince of Peace.

Of the increase of his government and peace
there will be no end.
He will reign on David's throne
and over his kingdom,
establishing and upholding it
with justice and righteousness
from that time on and for ever. (Isaiah 9:6-7)

Characters
Isaiah, a prophet
Two listeners, A and B; the listeners can be either sex, but it helps if B is male.

What did he say?

Isaiah stands in the pulpit if there is one. If not, he should be slightly removed from the other two.

Isaiah *(as dramatically as possible)* Surely wickedness burns like a fire; it consumes briars and thorns.

Enter A and B in a hurry. They both carry books. A is earnest and interested. B is bored.

A Come on, come on, I told you we'd be late.

B All right, all right. I don't know what all the fuss is about!

A *(pointing at Isaiah)* Isaiah has started already.

B And no doubt he'll be going for some time. Prophets aren't exactly known for their brevity, are they?

A He's got a good turnout. Why, there's Martha from down our road. *(waves)* Coo-ee, Martha.

B Do you mind. Everyone's looking now! *(stands casually and holds up book so that congregation can read the title for the first time: '1001 Things to do in a Dull Prophecy')*

A You're not going to read are you?

B You know I only came because there's nothing better to do on a Saturday afternoon. How long do you think it's going to be before someone invents football?

A *(sighing)* Ssh. I want to listen. *(takes notes)*

Isaiah Woe to the Assyrian, the rod of my anger, in whose hand is the club of my wrath!

B *(looks up from book)* Did he say club?

A *(still taking notes)* He's prophesying against the Assyrians.

B   Good for him. They're nothing but trouble, those Assyrians. They've taken over most of the country, wrecked the economy and I don't like some of the ideas they're pushing on us! Israel should be run by Israelites, that's what I say. *(goes back to reading)*

Isaiah   See the Lord, the Lord Almighty, will lop off the boughs with great power.

B   *(looking up again)* Sounds like he's prophesying against trees now. Has God got something against vegetation?

A   Very funny. You know the trees are symbolic. They stand for . . . Something!

Isaiah   A shoot will come up from the stump of Jesse; from his roots a Branch will bear fruit.

B   Jesse? I've never heard of a tree called Jesse.

A   Jesse was King David's father! Don't you know anything? He's saying that God is going to send us a new king descended from David.

B   The last thing we need is a new king. The ones we've got are bad enough. You know what, I want to choose who leads the country. We should all vote on it – that would be a novel idea. What do you think?

A   It'll never catch on. *(pause)* Don't you understand what Isaiah is saying? This new king is going to be different.

(B starts to listen to Isaiah)

Isaiah   The Spirit of the Lord will rest on him – the Spirit of wisdom and of understanding, the Spirit of counsel and of power, the Spirit of knowledge and of the fear of the Lord – and he will delight in the fear of the Lord.

A   See, that sort of king. Wisdom and understanding, that's the sort of king we need.

B   It certainly is, but can you really see it happening? Kings are only human like the rest of us, you know. Even the best of them is bound to have his faults.

A   But he'll be David's descendant!

B   What's that got to do with anything? If you remember, Rehoboam was David's grandson – the kingdom was split in two because of him. King Ahaz is David's descendant – and look at him. He sacrificed his own son in some religious ritual and now he's doing everything he can to suck up to the Assyrians. It's David's descendants that got us invaded in the first place, why would we want another one?

Isaiah   He will not judge by what he sees with his eyes, or decide by what he hears with his ears.

B   He's not going to be much use then, is he? What is he going to judge by, smell?

A   Will you listen?

Isaiah   . . . but with righteousness he will judge the needy, with justice he will give decisions for the poor of the earth.

A   Sounds wonderful.

Isaiah   Righteousness will be his belt and faithfulness the sash round his waist.

B   Sounds a bit cold to me!

Isaiah   The wolf will live with the lamb, the leopard will lie down with the goat, the calf and the lion and the yearling together; and a little child will lead them.

A   *(still taking notes)* Oh, how wonderful.

B   But not very likely, is it? I mean, I seem to remember David couldn't even persuade his children to get on with each other. But his descendant is going to reconcile the entire animal kingdom, apparently.

Isaiah   The infant will play near the hole of the cobra, and the young child put his hand into the viper's nest.

B   I blame the parents myself. They're obviously not keeping an eye on them.

Isaiah   They will neither harm nor destroy on all my holy mountain, for the earth will be full of the knowledge of the Lord as the waters cover the sea. In that day the Root of Jesse will stand as a banner for the peoples; the nations will rally to him, and his place of rest will be glorious. In that day the Lord will reach out his hand a second time to reclaim the remnant that is left of his people from Assyria, from Lower Egypt, from Upper Egypt, from Cush, from Elam, from Babylonia, from Hamath and from the islands of the sea. Amen. *(a brief pause and then Isaiah sits down)*

A   Oh, he's such a wonderful prophet, isn't he? No matter how difficult life gets, Isaiah is always here to remind us that God has never deserted us.

B   But how could what he said possibly happen? No human being is that perfect.

A   All I know is that God will do it somehow.

B   All I know is that if we're going to have such an ideal king, God's going to have to do it himself.

Can I have a word?

Theme
Joseph describes how he saw the events of Christmas.

Introduction
This drama was written to use in a carol service. It looks at the challenges that Joseph faced, in an attempt to get away from the way in which the nativity is so often seen as a kind of fairy tale. As it is quite long, an optional break is given. In the original version Gabriel wore a magnificent halo made of Christmas tree lights, which was very popular with the congregation. However, Gabriel has the key speech at the end of the drama, and it will lose its impact if he looks too ridiculous. If you would like Gabriel to dress up, an optional extra section is included to explain the removal of the halo for his second appearance.

Scripture reference
Matthew 1:18-2:14

This is how the birth of Jesus Christ came about: His mother Mary was pledged to be married to Joseph, but before they came together, she was found to be with child through the Holy Spirit. (Matthew 1:18)

Characters
Joseph
Mary, his fiancée/wife
Anna, his mother-in-law
Gabriel, an archangel

Can I have a word?

Joseph stands on one side. Mary, Anna and Gabriel should preferably be out of sight and only appear to hold their part of the conversation.

Joseph   I'd just like to point out, I didn't ask for any of this. Quite the contrary in fact. I had my life sorted just as I wanted it. I had a good home, family and friends close by and a nice little business. I liked my life. I trusted God and was at peace with the universe. It seemed to me, in those long ago days that now seem like they happened to someone else, that all I really lacked was a family of my own. And I was quite sure that Mary was the partner I needed. So when she said . . .

Mary   Joseph, can I have a word?

Joseph   *(still addressing the congregation)* . . . how was I to know how much life was going to change? It just doesn't occur to you, does it? . . .

Mary   *(interrupting)* Joseph, I really do need a word.

Joseph   *(turning to Mary)* Of course, Mary, my love.

Mary   Joseph, you might want to sit down for this.

Joseph   It's all right, Mary, you can't shock me. Overspent on the wedding plans have you?

Mary   Not quite.

Joseph   Want to invite a few more relatives?

Mary   No, it's not about the wedding.

Joseph   What's your mother done now?

Mary   It's not my mother, it's me. I'm pregnant.

Joseph   I think I need to sit down.

Mary   Yes, Joseph.

Joseph   Pregnant, how can you be pregnant? No don't answer that – I know how you can be pregnant.

Mary   It's not what you think.

Joseph   It's exactly what I think. There's only one way for a woman to get pregnant!

Mary   Don't you be so sure!

Exit Mary

Joseph   *(addressing congregation)* I really hadn't asked for that, had I? You have no idea what it was like. Half my friends assumed I was the father and thought I was a fool for not being more careful when I was with my fiancée. The other half assumed I wasn't the father and thought I was a fool for not being more careful in my choice of fiancée. I didn't want to hurt Mary, but why should I get landed with a baby that wasn't mine? So I started to make my plans to quietly cancel the wedding. You can understand, I'm sure, that I really wasn't ready for an angel to say . . .

Gabriel   Joseph, can I have a word?

Joseph   *(addressing congregation)* I mean this is not the sort of thing that happens to normal people, is it? One minute there I was comfortably in the land of nod and the next thing I know I'm face to face with this, this vision. You should have seen his wings, they were . . .

Gabriel   *(interrupting)* Joseph, I really do need a word.

Joseph   *(turning to Gabriel)* Of course, um . . .

Gabriel   Gabriel. Archangel Gabriel.

Joseph   Very glad to meet you, Mr Archangel, Sir.

Gabriel   Joseph, you might want to sit down for this.

Joseph   Oh that's all right. There's nothing left can shock me now.

Gabriel   You're to marry Mary.

Joseph   I think I need to sit down.

Gabriel   Yes, Joseph.

Joseph   You do know that she's um . . .

Gabriel   She's um?

Joseph   You know, how does the King James Bible put it, 'great with child'?

Gabriel   I hear she's not bad with teenagers as well.

Joseph   No, no, that's not what I mean. I mean, she's pregnant.

Gabriel   Yes, we know all about that.

Joseph   And it's not mine.

Gabriel   Yes, we know that too. You're still to marry her. The child is God's and we want you to be the father.

Exit Gabriel

Joseph   *(addressing congregation)* Well, I really hadn't asked for that, had I? But you don't argue with angels *(uncertainly),* do you? So I reorganised the wedding and began to look forward to a nice quiet life with Mary and the baby. If only I had known.

BREAK

Joseph   It was a bit of a rush, organising the wedding so suddenly. I'm sure you'll understand that afterwards I was ready for a bit of space, just me and Mary and time to get ready for the baby to come. I really wasn't ready for my mother-in-law to say . . .

Anna   Joseph, can I have a word?

Joseph	You do expect to be left alone after you get married, don't you . . .
Anna	*(interrupting)* Joseph, I really do need a word.
Joseph	Certainly, how can I help?
Anna	You might want to sit down for this.
Joseph	Trust me, after what I've gone through in the last few months, nothing could shock me any more.
Anna	There's going to be a census.
Joseph	A whatus?
Anna	A census. The Romans want to count everyone.
Joseph	Oh well, if it keeps them happy.
Anna	They want to count everyone in their home town. We all have to go back to where our family came from – in the next two months.
Joseph	But, but, my family's from Bethlehem; that's miles away.
Anna	There's lots of people will have to travel further than that.
Joseph	The baby's due at the end of next month. I wanted to be there for the birth.
Anna	Oh, I think we can guarantee you will be.
Joseph	What do you mean?
Anna	We've checked the rules. Mary has to go with you.
Joseph	But Mary doesn't come from Bethlehem!
Anna	What can I say, it's the first century, it's a very sexist time.
Joseph	What stupid idiot thought this up?
Anna	I believe the stupid idiot's name is Caesar Augustus.

Joseph   I think I need to sit down.

Anna   I'll see you when you get back.

Exit Anna

Joseph   *(addressing congregation)* So I made some new plans. What else could I do? Eighty miles and no public transport. I cannot tell you how difficult it was, and when we got there we discovered someone had forgotten to book the room. So there I was with a new wife and a new baby, contemplating another 80-mile trip to get home. I really didn't need any more bad news.

Gabriel   Joseph, can I have a word?

Joseph   *(addressing Gabriel)* That depends, will I have to sit down?

Gabriel   Probably.

Optional explanation of the disappearing halo in italics below

Joseph   *What happened to the halo?*

Gabriel   *Michael borrowed it to decorate the Christmas tree.*

Joseph   *What's a Christmas tree?*

Gabriel   *We decided to celebrate the Messiah's birth by decorating a tree. We really like it, in fact we might do it every year to mark his birthday. What do you think?*

Joseph   *It'll never catch on.*

Gabriel   *We'll see!*

Joseph   OK, so tell me, how are things going to get worse? There must be a way, though I can't see it. I've got a new baby, I'm miles from home, oh and by the way, who should I thank for the shepherds?

Gabriel   Me, I'm afraid.

Joseph   I don't want to complain Gabriel, but they did arrive just as we got the baby off to sleep. There were rather a lot of them and they were very excited, and it's a very small stable.

Gabriel   Sorry.

Joseph   I wouldn't have minded, but they had to explain why they had come. Which involved their own special rendition of the song of the heavenly host. It's a great pity none of them could actually sing. Still, at least they were better than the next lot who showed up.

Gabriel   The wise men? What possible objection could you have to visitors from the east?

Joseph   It would have been nice if one of them could have spoken English.

Gabriel   Joseph, you're a first-century, Middle-Eastern Jew – you can't speak English!

Joseph   All right, Aramaic. All I'm saying is that a little mutual under-standing would have helped. I don't think they had the least idea what was happening – do you know what they brought as presents for the baby?

Gabriel   Well, as I was saying, I really do need a word.

Joseph   Of course, things are going to get worse, aren't they? You have some other visitors up your sleeve, haven't you?

Gabriel   No.

Joseph   Caesar Augustus had another bright idea?

Gabriel   No

Joseph   Don't tell me, Mary has another little surprise for me.

Gabriel   No.

Joseph   So what is it then?

James   We know all the stories. So no one could say we haven't been listening.

John   Hey, I've even been listening to some of the weird stuff he's started coming out with in the last few days.

James   What, about how the Pharisees are actually going to catch him, you mean?

John   And he's going to suffer and get killed. *(shivers)* I don't know where he got that from.

James   That's it! Of course. Don't you see! That's what this was all about.

John   What, all this stuff with bright lights and Moses and Elijah and talking clouds?

James   Yes – think about what the cloud said. 'This is my Son, whom I love, with him I am well pleased.' Well, if God's so fond of Jesus, he's hardly going to let him get killed, is he? Obviously, God was telling us that everything's going to be all right and we don't have to worry about all this stuff Jesus has been talking about. God is going to look after him.

John   So, God was telling us that Jesus has got it wrong?

James   He didn't want us to worry, obviously.

John   And how does that fit in with telling us that we have to listen to Jesus? Doesn't that kind of imply that he ought to be listening to us?

James   *(pauses to think)* No, I must be right – no way is God going to let anything happen to Jesus. That would be crazy. Come on, let's go and tell the others. *(exit James)*

John   Listen to him, that's what the voice said – I just can't help but think that we are missing something. *(walks slowly off, in the same direction as James)*

Yes, Your Excellency

Theme

A civil servant tries to get Pilate to co-operate with the chief priests' plans for Jesus' death.

Introduction

This drama can be used at any point in Lent or Holy Week but is probably best suited to Palm Sunday or Maundy Thursday, perhaps with the last section used on Easter Day. Some optional breaks are marked so that it can be used in different services. It emphasises the biblical theme that Christ was an innocent man.

Scripture reference

Matthew 27:1-26

While Pilate was sitting on the judge's seat, his wife sent him this message: 'Don't have anything to do with that innocent man, for I have suffered a great deal today in a dream because of him.' But the chief priests and the elders persuaded the crowd to ask for Barabbas and to have Jesus executed. (Matthew 27:19-20)

Characters

Pilate, a Roman Governor
Humpheronus, his civil servant

Yes, Your Excellency

Pilate   *(addressing congregation)* I'd just like to say that it isn't easy being a Governor in the Roman Empire. And it is made especially difficult when you are sent to a little backwater like Israel. I knew I had only one option – I had to be a success. Judea had to become a co-operative, quiet, productive part of the Roman Empire. I would be tough but fair. I would not be afraid to make difficult decisions. I would be tough on rebellion and tough on the causes of rebellion. And then I knew Rome would take notice and I would make my name. I was determined that I, Pontius Pilate, would be remembered for years to come.

Enter Humpheronus.

Humph   Good morning, Your Excellency.

Pilate   Humpheronus, good morning. Do you have a report for me?

Humph   Everything is fairly quiet, sir. The Jews are occupied preparing for their latest festival. We have only a couple of problems at the moment. There seems to have been an outbreak of theft and we think the Jews have formed another sect.

Pilate   Well, that doesn't sound too bad. What has been stolen?

Humph   Palm branches, Your Excellency.

Pilate   Palm branches?

Humph   Yes, sir. Apparently, every tree in a two-mile radius has been stripped bare. The owners are furious.

Pilate   But who would steal palm branches?

Humph   We're not quite certain, sir.

Pilate   And the new sect?

Humph   Well, again we are still investigating. But our guards report a large number of Jews with hoof marks on their cloaks. We are

61

still trying to discover the religious significance of these marks. In fact, I'm just about to go and meet with some chief priests to see what information they can give us. If Your Excellency would excuse me?

Pilate   Of course.

Exit Humpheronus.

Pilate   *(addressing congregation)* I'm sure you can see my problem. They're an awkward lot, the Jews. They have very strange religious ideas; they will insist that there is only one God. Why, that's virtually atheism! And they had so many peculiar rules about what they could and couldn't do! I didn't understand them at all. But I knew my job as governor. I was Caesar's representative and, while we Romans are prepared to tolerate a great deal from those that we rule, in the end, my word was law. I just had to make sure that the Jews respected that.

Enter Humpheronus

Humph   I think I've got to the bottom of the problem, Your Excellency.

Pilate   Excellent!

Humph   It's Jesus of Nazareth, sir.

Together   *(looking at each other)* Again!

Pilate   *(wearily)* What's he done this time?

Humph   He got the crowd quite excited when he rode into Jerusalem. But according to the Pharisees that's not the real problem. What they really object to is his mode of transportation.

Pilate   They do?

Humph   Yes, sir, he was riding on a donkey.

Pilate   And that's a problem? Why? Don't tell me they've all joined the Jerusalem branch of the Donkey Protection League.

Humph   No, sir.

Pilate   I know – it's against the Jewish law to ride donkeys on a Sunday through a city gate!

Humph   No. Apparently it's one of their prophets. He said that the King of the Jews will arrive on a donkey. They're suggesting that we charge him with treason.

Pilate   Treason? It's going to be quite difficult to argue that one man riding a donkey is a major threat to the biggest army in the world, don't you think?

Humph   I did explain that to them, sir. So they suggested the lesser charge of donkey theft.

Pilate   It wasn't his donkey, I take it. So why don't you charge him?

Humph   He gave the donkey back. But we are still working on it.

Pilate   The chief priests really don't like this Jesus character, do they?

Humph   No, sir. They seem to think he poses some sort of danger to them.

Pilate   All right, Humpheronus, keep me informed.

Exit Humpheronus.

BREAK

Pilate   *(addressing congregation)* And that was the other problem with the Jews. They had this theory about a coming Messiah who was going to rescue them. A new Messiah kept turning up every couple of years or so, and the chief priests would get upset and expect me to deal with them. Jesus of Nazareth was just one more in a long line. So, here we were again. Passover in Jerusalem and another wandering prophet stirring things up. And the priests were expecting me to solve their problem for them. Well, sooner or later, someone had to put their foot down. And so, a couple of days later, I decided that was what I would do.

Enter Humpheronus.

Pilate	Humpheronus. I have something to tell you. I've decided that I've had enough of all the propaganda and lies. Tell the priests that it is quite clear that Jesus is an innocent man and I have no intention of being taken in by their manipulations. I know they won't like it, but they are going to have to live with it. I'm in charge around here and it's about time they recognised it.
Humph	Yes, Your Excellency. *(pause)* And how is Lady Pilate these days?
Pilate	*(sighs)* She's not sleeping. Which means that I'm not sleeping. Do you understand me?
Humph	I understand you perfectly. I've met Lady Pilate, remember?
Pilate	Yes, well. So you'll pass on to the Pharisees that my wife's . . . I mean my decision is final.
Humph	Of course, Your Excellency. Do I take it that you don't want to hear my report?
Pilate	I'm not going to change my mind. You do understand that?
Humph	I do.
Pilate	Well, I'm sure that it can't hurt just to hear the report.
Humph	Jesus has been out and about in Jerusalem once more. There is the usual crop of inexplicable stories. One of our spies says that he is smelling very strongly of expensive perfume, so the chief priests are hoping for a sex scandal. In addition they are very unhappy with some of the stories he's been telling.
Pilate	Why? Are the stories about them?
Humph	Well, the one that I heard was about a dispute over the owner-ship of a vineyard.
Pilate	He's not one of those radicals with no respect for ownership of property, is he?
Humph	In the story, the owner rented out the vineyard but the tenants refused to pay their rent. They even killed the owner's son when he went to get it.

Pilate   And I suppose Jesus thought that this was all right, did he?

Humph   No, sir. The story ended with the tenants being thrown out.

Pilate   So, right triumphed in the end. I hope those who killed the son got what they deserved?

Humph   I believe they did, sir.

Pilate   Quite right too. Well, I can't see their problem. So, what else has he done?

Humph   He turned some tables over in the Temple.

Pilate   Anything else?

Humph   The priests have requested that you have him executed, sir.

Pilate   Executed? What for? He hasn't murdered anyone, has he?

Humph   Well, there was this fig tree.

Pilate   Fig tree?

Humph   Yes, sir. Jesus was seen talking to a fig tree and a few minutes later it apparently withered away.

Pilate   What did he do, upset its feelings? So let me make sure I've got this straight. So far, the charges against him seem to be borrowing a donkey, smelling of perfume in a public place, the unauthorised rearrangement of ecclesiastical furniture and the murder of one fig tree. None of them are exactly capital offences, are they?

Humph   No. But the chief priests would quite like him executed anyway.

Pilate   Well, I'm not going to do it.

Humph   Of course, sir. They just thought that you might be interested to know that if you don't have Jesus executed, the people will riot.

Pause while Pilate thinks about this.

Pilate   That makes no difference to my decision.

Humph   That's very brave of you, sir.

Pilate   *(worried)* It is?

Humph   Yes. In view of the fact that the people have rioted twice before, and Rome did happen to mention that should there be another fracas you'll be recalled.

Pilate   *(worried)* But if I just give in to them, I'll look weak.

Humph   Disgraced former governors aren't given another job very often, are they, Your Excellency?

Pilate   The important point is that Jesus has not actually done anything wrong.

Humph   Absolutely, sir. And think how good it will be for you to leave politics and spend more time with Lady Pilate.

Pause.

Pilate   On the other hand, it would be a major risk to Rome's authority if we had another riot. And it is my job to prevent such threats taking place.

Humph   Just what I was thinking, Your Excellency.

Pilate   Hang on a minute. The people are going to riot. How do the Pharisees know that? They're not planning on arranging it, are they?

Humph   No, Your Excellency. Of course not. They just happen to know that a riot is going to spontaneously erupt *(pause)* in about five hours' time. *(pause)* Possibly.

Pilate   And this spontaneous riot may just happen to not take place if I execute Jesus for them?

Humph   That would be my assessment of the situation. They're bringing him here tonight, sir. For a trial.

Pilate   On what charge?

Humph   They haven't decided the charges yet, but they said to let you know that any verdict will do. *(pause)* As long as it's 'Guilty'.

Pilate   This is perversion of justice. This is appalling! I can't do it.

Humph   Indeed, sir. I'll just tell the chief priests that, shall I? It's just a shame it's Passover really.

Pilate   What do you mean?

Humph   Jerusalem is pretty crowded, with all those pilgrims who've arrived for the festival. If a riot should happen to spontaneously occur, they could do a lot of damage, *(pause)* especially to your reputation.

Pilate   Hang on a minute. I thought Jesus was popular with the common people. Perhaps they'll riot if I do arrest him. What do I do then?

Humph   The chief priests have already thought of that, sir. They know how important it is to you to keep the peace, so they said to tell you that they will make sure to arrest him quietly and there will be no trouble.

Pilate   And how are they going to do that?

Humph   I don't know, sir. But they said that their expenses would be a mere 30 pieces of silver. Very reasonable, I thought.

Pilate   I don't have any choice, do I?

Humph   *(sympathetically)* All politicians have to make difficult decisions, sir. It's just part of the job, I'm afraid.

Pilate   Come along then.

Humph   I'll just get the bowl of water.

Pilate   Bowl of water, what's that for?

Humph   Presiding over a trial is hard work. I just thought you might want to wash your hands at some point, Your Excellency.

Exit Humpheronus.

BREAK

Pilate   *(addressing congregation)* Strange things happen in my job. As governor of Judea I meet the most unlikely people. But somehow the one that sticks in my mind the most is Jesus of Nazareth. They'd beaten him, of course, even before he got to me. And, of course I had him flogged, to pacify those yelling for his death. But even with the blood running down his face, he looked me straight in the eye and I had this strange feeling that somehow he was more in control than I was. I wanted to save him. How I wanted to save him! But, politics is the art of the possible and I just couldn't. But even now, three days after his trial and death, I just keep thinking about him and wondering.

Enter Humpheronus.

Pilate   Good morning, Humpheronus.

Humph   Good morning, Your Excellency, and how are you today?

Pilate   I feel so much better this morning. It is such a relief to have the Jesus of Nazareth situation finally sorted out.

Pause; Humpheronus winces.

Humph   Ah, yes. About the Jesus of Nazareth situation. We seem to have a slight problem.

Pilate: We do?

Humph   We appear to be in a temporary cadaver deficiency situation, sir.

Pilate   Pardon?

Humph   We seem to have been accidentally downsized in the corpse department.

Pilate   I do wish you'd speak proper Latin, Humpheronus.

Humph   We've lost the body.

Silence.

Pilate   We've lost the body?

Humph   Yes, Your Excellency.

Pilate   This would be the body that we already buried, right?

Humph   Yes, Your Excellency.

Pilate   And put a whopping great big stone in front of the tomb?

Humph   Yes, Your Excellency.

Pilate   And then sealed it.

Humph   Yes, Your Excellency.

Pilate   And then, just for good measure, put two guards outside it?

Humph   Yes, Your Excellency.

Pilate   So what did it do? Get up and walk away by itself?

Humph   No, according to the guards it had some help, sir. There was an earthquake and two angels who rolled the stone away. *(pause)* And then it got up and walked away by itself.

Pilate   It did?

Humph   Apparently, sir.

Pilate   Were these guards sober?

Humph   It seems so, sir.

Pilate   Awake?

Humph   Unfortunately, yes, sir.

Pilate   And how do you suggest that I explain this one to Rome? 'Dear Caesar, crucifixion didn't work. Can I borrow a couple of lions, please?'

Humph   It might be difficult to throw him to the lions, sir. We don't know where he is. We could try it with some of his followers though!

Pilate	You are missing the point. How am I going to explain this mess to Rome?
Humph	At the moment our preferred option is suggesting that his disciples stole the body.
Pilate	That's good. No, hang on a minute, we can't say that. People will think that a bunch of illiterate peasants outwitted my trained soldiers!
Humph	In that case, sir, we'll have to go with Plan B.
Pilate	And what is Plan B?
Humph	You write to Rome and tell them that we appear to have accidentally crucified the Son of God and do they have any advice. In the same letter you could inquire after Caesar's horse.
Pilate	Caesar's horse?
Humph	Yes, sir. We're going to need something pretty big to bury this story. If, for example, Caesar were to give his horse a seat in the Senate, that might distract people.
Pilate	It's not very likely though, is it?
Humph	No, Your Excellency.
Pilate	*(trying the story out)* His disciples stole the body. *(pause)* Of course some of these illiterate peasants can be very clever. Education isn't everything, Humpheronus.
Humph	Yes, Your Excellency.
Pilate	You're right. We'll just say that his disciples stole the body. And then we'd better hope that it just dies down soon. After all, Humpheronus, a week is a long time in politics. With a bit of luck, in a couple of months, no one will remember this Jesus character.
Humph	Yes, Your Excellency.

The family business

Theme

Jesus' brothers are less than happy about his new career move.

Introduction

This drama could possibly be used to look at the events of the wedding at Cana, but its main theme is the demands which Jesus made on his family, leading to a wider exploration of the cost of discipleship.

Scripture reference

Mark 3:20–35

When his family heard about this, they went to take charge of him, for they said, 'He is out of his mind.' (Mark 3:21)

Characters

James, brother of Jesus
Simon, brother of Jesus
Mary, mother of Jesus

The family business

Enter James carrying a container, which he places on the desk. Enter Simon carrying a large sign, facing away from the audience.

Simon I've done it, what do you think? *(holds up sign so that it is facing James but the audience cannot see it)*

James *(uncertainly)* Well . . .

Simon *(looking at James' container)* Is that the biggest one you can find?

James There's more outside!

Enter Mary carrying a large empty box, marked 'Confetti'. James and Simon try to hide the sign and container.

Mary Well, that was a lovely wedding, wasn't it? But what are you two doing here? Why aren't you back at work?

Simon and James exchange glances.

Simon We've been meaning to talk to you about that, Mum.

Mary You have?

James We're just wondering if carpentry is really us. I keep getting splinters in my hands.

Simon And I'm sure I'm allergic to the dust.

James I'm definitely allergic to hitting my thumb with the hammer; it brings me out in great big bruises!

Simon And now that it looks like Jesus will be leaving the business.

Mary Jesus is just having a bit of time off, that doesn't mean he's leaving.

James *(sighing)* Mum, face facts. Jesus has got some weird ideas these days, he's not coming back to the family business.

Mary	I don't know what you mean!
Simon	Look at last month, there we were with loads of work to do and Jesus disappears for 40 days. Comes back muttering about turning stones into bread and jumping off high buildings. I mean it's not exactly normal, is it?
James	And he has been hanging out with John a lot recently. That's enough to give anybody strange ideas.
Mary	You two are very unfair to your cousin.
Simon	Unfair? Us unfair? Mum, do you have any idea what it's like being known as John's cousin in this village? Only last week I asked that nice Sarah if she wanted to come back for tea and all she said in reply was, 'Will there be locusts on the menu?'
James	You think you've got problems!
Mary	Not this again. I've told you before, James, your middle name is a reminder of where you were born.
Simon	Although you never have explained why a family from Nazareth spent a couple of years in Egypt of all places!
James	And being called James Tutankhamen Josephson does not exactly help someone fit in around here!
Simon	Anyway, as I was saying, it's not easy being John's cousin!
James	And now Jesus looks like he's going the same way!
Simon	Although, on the other hand, have you met his new friends? They're the most unreligious bunch I've come across in a long time. I can't really imagine Peter in a synagogue. Or James and John for that matter, they'd stick out a mile!
James	Yeah, the smell of fish might have something to do with it. But don't forget, they won't let John in any of the synagogues either. Apparently the Pharisees took offence at being called a bunch of snakes, can't think why!

Mary   (*doubtfully*) You don't think Jesus would ever upset people like that, do you?

James   Who knows, Mum. So that's why Simon and I think that we need to keep a careful eye on him.

Simon   And have another think about the family business at the same time.

James   After all, Jesus is clearly developing other interests and, as his brothers, we think that we should encourage him.

Mary   But you just said . . .

Simon   In some of them. Not the religious ones obviously. We were thinking more about his new business venture.

Mary   What new business venture? Is he going to start fishing with Peter?

James   No, it was the wedding that gave us the idea.

Simon   We thought we might get into the catering business. What do you think? (*turns the sign around so that Mary and the congregation can read it – 'Joseph and Sons: Carpenters'; the word Carpenters has been crossed out and written in by hand are the words, 'Wine Sellers'*)

That day

Theme
A disciple, a member of the crowd and a Pharisee describe the events of Palm Sunday.

Introduction
These meditations were written to replace the sermon for a reflective service.

Scripture reference
Mark 11:1-11

Many people spread their cloaks on the road, while others spread branches they had cut in the fields. Those who went ahead and those who followed shouted, 'Hosanna! Blessed is he who comes in the name of the Lord!' 'Blessed is the coming kingdom of our father David!' 'Hosanna in the highest!' Jesus entered Jerusalem and went to the Temple. He looked around at everything, but since it was already late, he went out to Bethany with the Twelve. (Mark 11: 8-11)

Characters
Disciple
Onlooker
Pharisee

That day

Disciple   I had such high hopes that day.

Looking back I can't quite remember how it started. Some of it is quite clear in my mind. I remember that the Lord sent two of us off to find the donkey. It was all a little secretive, go to this village and just take the colt. If anyone challenged us all we had to say was, 'The Lord needs it.' I had my doubts. Between you and me I had visions of being arrested for donkey theft; but sure enough, when the owner turned up and wanted to know what we were doing, all we said was, 'The Lord needs it', and he seemed quite happy. I never did work out if Jesus had set it all up beforehand, and if he had, how? When did he have time to search an unknown village for someone willing to lend us a donkey? Anyway, that bit I do remember. But what I can never quite figure out now is, who started the shouting? Who decided that we should spread our cloaks before him? And who first started pulling branches off the palm trees? That's all a bit of a blank really. But, somehow or other, that's what we ended up doing. Shouting, waving, making a real fuss.

And I was so excited. I know that part of the excitement was just being part of the crowd, but it was more than that – so much more. It felt like, this was what we had been leading up to all these years. This was going to make all the sacrifices, all the heartache, worthwhile. Jesus was finally going to be recognised for the King that he was and I was one of the inner circle. At that moment I was so glad that I had responded to the call; I was so glad that I had left everything behind and gone with him. I didn't care any more about the nights when there was nowhere to sleep, the days when I wondered just how he could possibly feed us all. I didn't even care about the parables that I couldn't understand and the miracles that I could never quite manage to imitate. Nothing mattered any more because we had finally made it. The crowd were with us, the Pharisees powerless to stop us, and so I shouted with the best of them.

And I can never quite remember either, how he let it all slip away. When did he stop being the crowd's favourite and become an object of scorn? At what point in the week did Barabbas replace him in the crowd's affections? And when did the Pharisees, who seemed so weak on the Sunday, decide that they could safely arrest him on the Thursday? I look back and I just can't quite remember, just can't quite believe that it happened that way.

I had such high hopes that day.

Onlooker It was a strange day.

OK, I admit it, I'd never heard of him before.

It was my first pilgrimage to Jerusalem. I'd always promised myself that one day I would celebrate the Passover there. It's the dream of every Jew I guess, to celebrate the holiest feast in the holiest city. But I live in Corinth and Jerusalem is a long way from home. Who has the time or the resources to travel hundreds of miles every Passover? But I promised myself, once, just once in my lifetime, I would make the pilgrimage and my Passover lamb would really have been slaughtered in the Temple, just like the Law says.

So there I was, my first time in the Holy City. I was lucky – a very distant cousin lived there and was willing to put me up. There were several days to go before Passover itself, so I was taking the chance to see the sights. I was standing on the walls, looking down on the Kidron Valley, when I saw them. They were the other side of the valley, coming down the Mount of Olives, just a small group of people, but they were making some noise I can tell you. And there in the middle was someone who was obviously important. I could tell he was riding something, but from that distance I couldn't see what. For a while I stood and watched as they got closer. Their excitement was contagious, and I began to feel it too. Someone important was arriving in the Holy City and I was there to see it! So I ran, down the steps and along to the gate. I came out of the gate just as they were starting up the path from the bottom of the valley. Now I could see that they were waving palm branches and I could hear what they were shouting: 'Hosanna to the Son of David,' and 'Blessed is the King who comes in the name of the Lord.' And so you know, at the time I thought, 'The King, the King is here, and I'm going to see him!' It was much later before I thought to wonder about a king I'd never heard of.

So I ran to the nearest tree and pulled off a branch and joined in. I found myself shouting with the rest of them, waving my branch, urging others to join in. I put my cloak on the ground, just like the rest of them. Ended up with hoof marks on it that never did come out. I didn't even stop shouting when I noticed that this so-called king didn't even have so much as a horse. A donkey, that's what he was riding. I ask you, what sort of king rides a donkey?

In the end it just sort of petered out. He entered the city and seemed to head off in the direction of the Temple and we were left, holding our palm branches and looking at each other a little sheepishly.

I celebrated that Passover with my cousin as planned. I heard later that this so-called king lasted about a week. The authorities stamped down on him – not surprising really, you can't have people going about crowning themselves, can you? So that was the end of that really.

But every so often I find myself looking back and thinking – it was a strange day.

Pharisee We came very close to a major catastrophe that day.

I was in the Temple courts, with a couple of the scribes. It was the usual Passover problems, people who had arrived late and were complaining there was no accommodation left. Someone else who had brought a sub-standard lamb and just wouldn't understand why we wouldn't allow it to be sacrificed. Just one more ordinary day in the Temple really.

And then a lad arrived, in a terrible rush. Caiaphas wanted to see me straightaway, because there was trouble brewing. And when the High Priest calls, you don't ask questions.

I found Caiaphas on the walls, looking down on the Kidron Valley. I could hear the noise before I even reached him; he didn't need to tell me what the problem was. There they were, a mob. An undisciplined, raucous, over-excited mob. They were rushing around, vandalising trees, shouting at the top of their voices. And in the middle of it all was him. Calm as could be, he was. Sat on an ass and yet looking more regal than Herod ever seemed. Well, of course I didn't need Caiaphas to remind me what the prophet Zechariah had said: 'Rejoice, O daughter of Zion! See your King comes to you, righteous and having salvation, gentle and riding on a donkey, on a colt, the foal of a donkey.' And here he was quite deliberately pretending that he could fulfil a scriptural prophecy. I doubt a single member of that undereducated mob understood what he was doing, but I knew. Anyone who knew their

Scriptures would find it difficult to miss. And as he passed beneath us he looked me straight in the eye and I knew, I knew that he understood precisely what he was doing, who he was claiming to be.

Beside me I heard Caiaphas mutter, 'He's gone too far this time.' And I agreed with him. The last thing we needed was people running around announcing the Messiah had come and had entered the city in triumph. The Romans would never have stood for it. It was obvious that something had to be done and done quickly.

I'll always be grateful that Caiaphas was a strong leader and was prepared to do what had to be done. It was messy of course. Pilate was as obstinate as ever and it took some time to persuade him that really he had no choice. And there were those who thought we went too far. 'Why didn't you just reason with him?' they asked. 'Why not sit down and talk to him, show him the error of his ways?' As if you can reason with a fanatic!

But I look back and shudder at how close it all was; I don't like to think about what could have been. We came very close to a major catastrophe that day.

The new parents

Theme
Mary and Joseph discuss the problems involved in parenting God's Son.

Introduction
A drama for the Sunday after Christmas. Most first-time parents are a little nervous about their new responsibilities. This drama suggests that Mary and Joseph had reason to be more nervous than most.

Scripture reference
Luke 2:1-24

When the time of their purification according to the Law of Moses had been completed, Joseph and Mary took him to Jerusalem to present him to the Lord (as it is written in the Law of the Lord, 'Every firstborn male is to be consecrated to the Lord'), and to offer a sacrifice in keeping with what is said in the Law of the Lord: 'a pair of doves or two young pigeons'. (Luke 2:22-24)

Characters
Joseph
Mary

Never again will I come down from a mountainside where I have touched Heaven and hear Peter, James and John locked in one more argument about their own importance. I have finished with all of that. But my love for them will never end.

It is ended. The greatest battle of all is done. I have faced the liars and the petty politicians and they have done their worst. I have taken the beatings and the contempt, the night of false accusations and the dawn, which brought execution. I have carried my cross through the mocking crowds and born the agony and the loneliness of crucifixion. I have cried out to a silent God and heard only my critics' voices in reply. It is finished.

And now the new life begins.

Questions

Theme
Peter, Judas and Mary describe their feelings after Good Friday.

Introduction
The following meditations were written to introduce an Easter morning service. They seek to express something of what Peter, Judas and Mary may have felt, while deliberately making their questions as universal as possible. The rest of the service was then a celebration of the risen Lord who welcomes us all to follow him, no matter what our doubts or struggles.

Characters
Peter
Mary
Judas

Questions

Peter   Will one mistake always haunt me?

I wonder – will I always be known as the person who denied Jesus Christ? I feel like I will never escape the guilt. It's only been a day or so, but already I wonder if that was the defining moment of my life. The day I forgot everything I valued most and did something that I never thought I would do.

The question is – does that one false step outweigh all the good I ever did? Does it make me a bad person? Yes, I found him difficult to understand, yes, he sometimes seemed very disappointed in me. But I followed him, didn't I? I stuck by him when it was obvious trouble was coming, didn't I? I gave up an entire life and put up with sleepless nights, not knowing where the next meal was coming from. I'm only human and of course I enjoyed the admiration from others, the people who seemed a bit awe-struck to meet one of his friends. But that's not much, in comparison with everything I gave up and every-thing I put up with.

Even when it was obvious that it was all over – I still tried. Which is more than anyone else can say. It was only when I had gone as far as I could and I saw no other way out – that I said the words I will always regret. One mistake and it feels like it will haunt me for the rest of my life.

Mary   Why is life so complicated?

At first it was so simple. He was the first man I ever met who seemed to treat me as a real person – and so I loved him, it really was that simple. All I wanted was a little of his time, a chance to support him. I didn't ask much. I just wanted to sit and listen as he talked about God and how much God loves us. I wanted to watch as someone else was healed or touched or had their whole life restored to them. I wanted to be one of his friends – one of those closest to him. I didn't ask much. And at first, it seemed I could have what I wanted. It was easy and it was beautiful.

But then it all got so complicated. I never understood why he had to deliberately provoke arguments with the wrong people. Why couldn't he just keep his head down? Why couldn't he sometimes just back away when they challenged him? We're just simple country folk and he had to go and take on the rich and the powerful. The more they argued, the more bewildered I became. Then he insisted he had to go to Jerusalem, even though everyone warned him not to. I wonder now – did I ever understand him?

And so all our dreams are shattered; the only person I ever really loved is gone and I don't understand why. Why is life so complicated? It wasn't much that I asked for – just to be with him. What harm did he ever really do? Why is it so often the good people who get hurt? Why, why, why?

Judas   Why wouldn't he do as I said?

It needn't have come to this. The others will blame me, but it's not my fault. All he had to do was listen to me and bend a little more. Be a little more willing to tell the priests and the Pharisees what they wanted to hear, keep his voice down on the controversial questions.

But he was so sure that he was right. In his Father's kingdom the first would be last and the last first, and that's what he told anyone who would listen. Then he wondered why the authorities got upset.

We could have done very nicely. He was popular, a very good speaker, and he'd begun to attract some wealthier followers. We could have made some real money, carried on for a few years and then quietly retired with some real security. Lord knows, there are few enough ways for people like us to escape the poverty around here.

But he just wouldn't listen. He knew what was right and nothing I said was going to make any difference. 'You can't serve God and money,' he kept insisting. And he had to serve God. He had to carry on, no matter whom he upset. Everything was so black and white. All he had to do was compromise a little. I just don't understand why he wouldn't listen to me.

The AGM

Theme

It's the first Annual General Meeting of the Church in Damascus and Ananias would like to propose a new member.

Introduction

An introduction to the story of Saul's conversion which highlights the difficulties faced by the early Church. It is important that the women make it clear that they are ganging up on Ananias. The Methodist terms can, of course, be changed to those appropriate to other denominations.

Scripture reference

Acts 9:1-19

The Lord told him, 'Go to the house of Judas on Straight Street and ask for a man from Tarsus named Saul, for he is praying. In a vision he has seen a man named Ananias come and place his hands on him to restore his sight.'

'Lord,' Ananias answered, 'I have heard many reports about this man and all the harm he has done to your saints in Jerusalem. And he has come here with authority from the chief priests to arrest all who call on your name.'

But the Lord said to Ananias, 'Go! This man is my chosen instrument to carry my name before the Gentiles and their kings and before the people of Israel. I will show him how much he must suffer for my name.' (Acts 9:11-15)

Characters

Ananias
Tabitha, secretary of the AGM
Rachael

The AGM

Rachael sits at the head of a table with Tabitha to one side. Tabitha has a pad of paper and there are a number of empty chairs around the table. Enter Ananias.

Rachael Evening, Ananias.

Ananias Good evening, I'm sorry I'm late.

Rachael Never mind, I'm delighted to see you. *(she moves chairs)* Do have a seat. *(she gestures to the one she has just vacated)*

Ananias I'm sorry? You want me to chair the meeting.

Tabitha *(as if this is obvious)* Well, of course. You're a man.

Ananias So?

Tabitha It's the first century and a woman couldn't possibly chair a meeting if a man is present.

Rachael *(nodding)* It's a very sexist time. I wouldn't dream of taking a job away from a man.

Pause while Rachael and Tabitha smile hopefully at Ananias, who knows he is being conned.

Ananias Oh, all right then. *(he sits in the chair that Tabitha vacated)*

Tabitha Here's the agenda. *(she hands him a piece of paper)*

Ananias *(reading)* The first Annual General Meeting of the Church in Damascus. Item One: Apologies for Absence.

Tabitha *(reading from another piece of paper)* We've received the following apologies. David is in jail, Andreas is in jail and Bartholomew is in jail.

Rachael Mary sends her apologies.

Ananias Don't tell me, she's in jail, right?

Rachael	No, Phillip arrived from Jerusalem. She went for a walk with him and the Spirit of the Lord took them both away. She's on her way back from Caesarea at the moment.
Ananias	Anyone else?
Tabitha	Bartimaeus is unlikely to join us, since he was stoned to death last week. Simon is in jail and Jonathon is on his way to Jerusalem.
Ananias	Why is he going there?
Tabitha	To be put in jail.
Rachael	Sarah sends her apologies.
Ananias	Jail?
Rachael	Toothache.
Ananias	So it's just the three of us then. *(reads from the agenda)* And the next item is 'The Minutes of the last meeting'. *(he looks at Tabitha)*
Tabitha	That's what you always have at an AGM.
Ananias	*(sighs and reads again)* Item Three: Property Report.
Rachael	*(happily)* We don't have any.
Ananias	*(getting a little annoyed)* Item Four: Financial Report.
Tabitha	*(happily)* We did have 20 pieces of silver but the authorities raided us, so now we don't have any money either.
Ananias	*(a little more annoyed)* Item Five: Election of Officers.
Tabitha	We need a steward.
Ananias	And who can be a steward?
Tabitha	Well, obviously it needs to be a man.

Rachael   Obviously. And I think it's really important that the steward should not be in jail.

Tabitha   So do I. *(they both look at Ananias)*

Ananias   *(pause and then sighs)* Oh, all right then.

Rachael   *(brightly)* Excellent. What's the next item on the agenda?

Ananias   Date of next meeting. Who wrote this agenda?

Tabitha   I just put in what you always have at an AGM.

Ananias   Well, there are some important things we need to discuss.

Rachael   *(interrupting him)* There certainly are. I think we should discuss what we are going to do about Saul of Tarsus.

Tabitha   Is it true that he's on his way to Damascus?

Rachael   That's what I heard. He's had Christians in Jerusalem stoned and thrown into jail and now he is on his way here.

Ananias   I don't think he ever actually had someone stoned.

Rachael   What about Stephen?

Ananias   He was there. But he didn't actually . . .

Tabitha   *(interrupting him)* Exactly, he's an evil man and he is on his way here.

Ananias   He might change his mind.

Rachael   A leopard doesn't change his spots.

Tabitha   And a leopard would be positively friendly compared with Saul of Tarsus.

Ananias   But what if something made him think?

Rachael   Think? Saul of Tarsus? The man could be struck by lightning and he wouldn't change his mind.

Tabitha   God could hit him with a bolt of light.

Rachael   Knock him off his horse.

Tabitha   Even strike him blind and it wouldn't make any difference.

Ananias   I'm not so sure.

Rachael   He's prejudiced; he hates us and that is all there is to it. Now what are we going to do?

Tabitha   We could appeal to the United Nations, tell them that we are a persecuted minority.

Ananias   Great idea, after all, there's less than 2000 years to go before they are founded.

Rachael   *(who has just thought of this)* I know! We could start a petition. We could collect lots of signatures and give it to the authorities.

Tabitha   Oh yes, that's a good idea. Now of course it will have to be a man who actually collects the signatures.

Rachael   Of course, after all, no woman could approach a man she doesn't know.

Pause while they both look hopefully at Ananias.

Ananias   We're an underground Church, remember. Are you sure you want to hand the authorities the name and address of everyone in Damascus who supports Christianity?

Tabitha   *(upset at Ananias's attitude)* Well then, do you have any bright ideas?

Ananias   *(not sure how to explain)* I, um, well. You see, I, *(pause)* I'd like to propose a new member.

Rachael   Oh wonderful. Is it anyone we know?

The women look interested, Ananias looks embarrassed and they all freeze.